The Wild World of Animals

Badgers

Active at Night

by Fran Howard

Consultant:
Marsha A. Sovada, PhD
Research Wildlife Biologist
Northern Prairie Wildlife Research Center
Jamestown, North Dakota

Bridgestone Books
an imprint of Capstone Press
Mankato, Minnesota

Bridgestone Books are published by Capstone Press
151 Good Counsel Drive, P.O. Box 669, Mankato, Minnesota 56002
www.capstonepress.com

Library of Congress Cataloging-in-Publication Data
Howard, Fran, 1953–
    Badgers: active at night / by Fran Howard.
    p. cm.—(The wild world of animals)
    Includes bibliographical references and index.
    Contents: Badgers—Where badgers live—Burrows—Night hunters—What badgers
eat—Family life—Cubs—Predators—People and badgers—Hands on: finding food.
    ISBN-13: 978-0-7368-2612-9 (hardcover)   ISBN-10: 0-7368-2612-2 (hardcover)
    1. Badgers—Juvenile literature. [1. Badgers.] I. Title. II. Series.
QL737.C25H68 2005
599.76'7—dc22   2003025825

Editorial Credits

Blake A. Hoena, editor; Linda Clavel, designer; Scott Thoms, photo researcher;
    Eric Kudalis, product planning editor

Photo Credits

Bruce Coleman Inc./Lee Lyon, 12
Cheryl A. Ertelt, 20
Comstock, 1
Corbis/Nigel J. Dennis/Gallo Images, 6; W. Perry Conway, cover
Erwin and Peggy Bauer, 16
Frederick D. Atwood, 4
McDonald Wildlife Photography/Joe McDonald, 8
naturepl.com/Kevin J Keatley, 10, 14
Tom Stack & Associates/Joe McDonald, 18

1 2 3 4 5 6 09 08 07 06 05 04

Table of Contents

Badgers 5

Where Badgers Live 7

Burrows 9

Night Hunters 11

What Badgers Eat 13

Family Life 15

Cubs 17

Predators 19

People and Badgers 21

Hands On: Finding Food 22

Glossary 23

Read More 24

Internet Sites 24

Index 24

white stripe

American badger

4

Badgers

Badgers are **mammals** with flat bodies and short, strong legs. They have white stripes down the middle of their faces. Badgers can be more than 2 feet (.6 meters) long and weigh up to 25 pounds (11 kilograms). Eight kinds of badgers live in the world.

honey badger

Where Badgers Live

Badgers live in many habitats. They live in grasslands, deserts, and forests. They also can be found near farms. American badgers live in the United States, Canada, and Mexico. Other kinds of badgers live in Europe, Africa, and Asia.

habitat
the place and natural conditions in which an animal lives

American badger

Burrows

Badgers spend most of their time underground. They live in burrows. Badgers use the sharp claws on their front feet to dig burrows. Most burrows are 12 feet (3.7 meters) deep. They can be 50 feet (15 meters) long.

burrow

a tunnel or hole in the ground used by an animal

Eurasian badger

Night Hunters

Badgers sleep during the day. They are **nocturnal**. They hunt for food at night. Badgers do not see as well as people do. They use their keen sense of smell to find food.

keen
able to notice things easily

Honey guide birds help honey badgers find food. Badgers follow the birds to beehives. The badgers break open the hives to get honey. The birds eat any leftover honey.

honey badger

What Badgers Eat

Badgers eat many types of food. They eat insects, birds, frogs, snakes, and lizards. American badgers hunt small animals, such as mice and gophers. Eurasian badgers dig for worms. Honey badgers eat fruit and honey.

Eurasian badger clan

Family Life

Some kinds of badgers live in family groups called **clans**. A clan includes **male** and **female** badgers and their cubs. Other types of badgers live alone. Males and females only come together to mate.

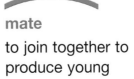

mate
to join together to produce young

American badger cub

Cubs

Female badgers have between one and four cubs. Cubs first leave the burrow when they are about 2 months old. Badger cubs learn to hunt from their mothers.

American badger

18

Predators

Badgers have few **predators**. Badgers are fierce animals. They have strong claws and sharp teeth. Most animals stay away from badgers. Wolf packs may attack badgers. Coyotes and eagles sometimes eat badger cubs.

American badger

People and Badgers

People do not see badgers very often. Badgers stay away from people. Some farmers like badgers because they eat mice and gophers. Other farmers do not like badgers because they dig burrows in fields. Some people trap badgers for their fur.

Hands On: Finding Food

Badgers find food using their keen sense of smell. Try this activity with friends to see if you can find food using your sense of smell.

What You Need

3 food items with a strong odor, such as orange slices, garlic cloves, and pepperoni slices
3 nonfood items with a strong odor, such as pine needles, crayons, and dirt
6 small plastic containers that you cannot see through
6 pieces of masking tape
Pen or pencil
6 pieces of odorless gauze
6 rubber bands

What You Do

1. Put each item into one of the six plastic containers.
2. Place a piece of masking tape on the bottom of each container. On the tape, write the name of the item that is in the container.
3. Cover each container with odorless gauze. Use a rubber band to hold the gauze in place.
4. Mix up the containers. Then take turns sniffing the containers to find the food items.

Glossary

clan (KLAN)—a large family group

female (FEE-male)—an animal of the sex that can give birth to young animals

male (MALE)—an animal of the sex that can father young animals

mammal (MAM-uhl)—a warm-blooded animal with a backbone and hair; female mammals produce milk to feed their young.

nocturnal (nok-TUR-nuhl)—active at night

predator (PRED-uh-tur)—an animal that hunts other animals for food

Read More

Butterfield, Moira. *Animals on Plains and Prairies.* Looking At. Austin, Texas: Raintree Steck-Vaughn, 2000.

Murphy, Patricia J. *Badgers.* Grassland Animals. Mankato, Minn.: Capstone Press, 2004.

Taylor, Barbara. *Night Animals.* Animal Close-ups. Columbus, Ohio: Peter Bedrick Books, 2003.

Internet Sites

FactHound offers a safe, fun way to find Internet sites related to this book. All of the sites on FactHound have been researched by our staff.

Here's how:
1. Visit *www.facthound.com*
2. Type in this special code **0736826122** for age-appropriate sites. Or enter a search word related to this book for a more general search.
3. Click on the **Fetch It** button.

FactHound will fetch the best sites for you!

Index

burrows, 9, 17, 21
clans, 15
claws, 9, 19
cubs, 15, 17 ,19
food, 11, 13, 21

habitats, 7
people, 21
predators, 19
sense of smell, 11
size, 5

DATE DUE